nancy brady

Ohayo Haiku

Drinian Press/
Huron, Ohio

Ohayo Haiku

Copyright © 2006 by Nancy Brady. All rights reserved. Except for use in a review, no part of this book may be reproduced or utilized in any form or by any means electronic or mechanical without written permission of the author c/o Drinian Press, P.O. Box 63, Huron, Ohio 44839.

Visit us online at www.DrinianPress.com.

Cover design © 2006 Drinian Press.

Japanese script by Yasumi Miyazawa

ISBN 0-9785165-3-2

1. Poetry   2. Haiku.

DrinianPress.com
Printed in the U.S.A.

Mom and Dad

おはよう

ohayo—greetings
haiku from the Midwest
Ohio, my home

生

Birth

Ohayo Haiku

splashes of purple
peek out of dark woods
soon covered in green

Ohayo Haiku

light filters through
dappled leaves of varied green
shades mossy grass

Ohayo Haiku

pale orb in the sky
burns away wisps of fog
sudden clarity

Ohayo Haiku

yellow lion's head
turns into a puffball
breath scatters seeds

Ohayo Haiku

red bud in bloom
purple flowers peek out
arrival of spring

Ohayo Haiku

cold and snow
crocus blooms open
hope of spring

Ohayo Haiku

tender buds on trees
burst into fragile leaves
verdant spring

Ohayo Haiku

milkweed pods open
seeds scatter on the wind
to new life

Ohayo Haiku

the water eddies
trees surf down river in
the storm's aftermath

Ohayo Haiku

pale moon
shines down on two lovers
a warm embrace

Ohayo Haiku

silhouetted trees
against an amber sky
deepening shadows

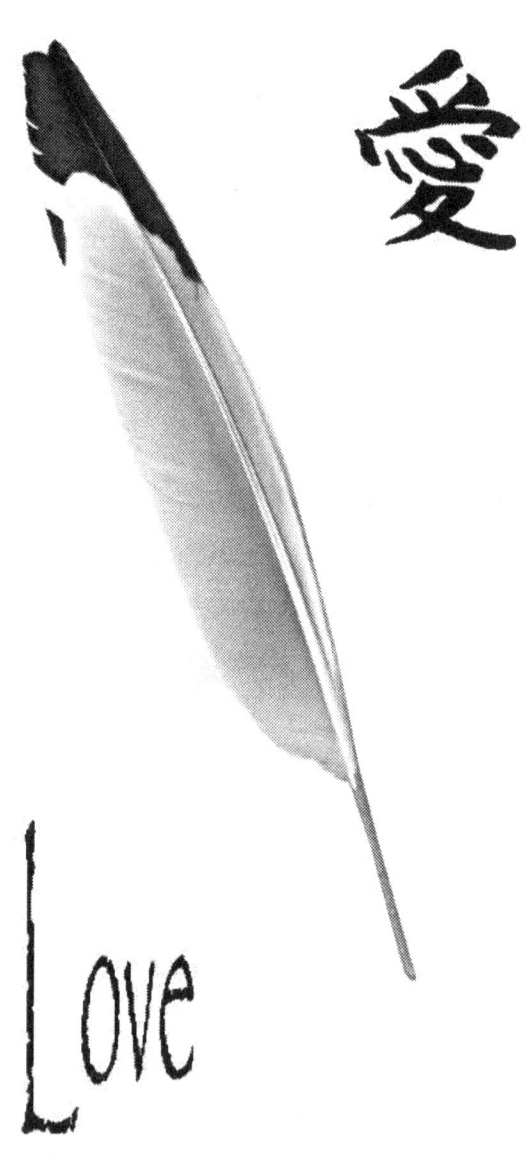

Ohayo Haiku

white clouds, azure skies
sunlight sparkles on the water
peaceful harbor

Ohayo Haiku

cocoa butter smells--
beach with warm sand and sun,
one lone figure bakes

Ohayo Haiku

the breeze on my toes
gently tickles memories
of summers gone by

Ohayo Haiku

radiant sunlight
masts-cathedral to the sky
sacred memory

Ohayo Haiku

a mist rises
on the hot, steamy asphalt
rains have ceased

Ohayo Haiku

waves whip the bow
spray flies over the rail
wets feet and toes

Ohayo Haiku

waves lap gently
where the water meets the shore
earth cycles anew

Ohayo Haiku

bright monkey faces
velvety purples and creams
gracing the garden

Ohayo Haiku

bright stars, night sky
water lapping at the bow
time of peace and dreams

Ohayo Haiku

riotous colors
blue, red, purple, and yellow
amid green grasses

Ohayo Haiku

great blue on the rocks
majestic gaze that surveys
his domain, the lake

哲

Wisdom

Ohayo Haiku

trees of red and gold
tucked between boughs of green
seasonal changes

Ohayo Haiku

golden sun rises
casting a coppery glow
upon sky, trees, earth

Ohayo Haiku

a mist is rising
river shrouded in silver
dawn at Lake Erie

Ohayo Haiku

crispness in the air
red, yellow, orange, and brown
falling leaves

Ohayo Haiku

riding on thermals
steely gaze watches for prey
red-tailed hawk

Ohayo Haiku

night skies overhead
an inky blackness dotted
by thousands of stars

Ohayo Haiku

quiet strumming
artists and poets listen
coffeehouse blues

Ohayo Haiku

the golden sun
casts a coppery glow
warming trees and earth

Ohayo Haiku

bright crimson and gold
dappled with shades of green
early fall palette

Ohayo Haiku

ducks on the river
gather and remind others
of the trip south

Ohayo Haiku

trees of green
painted with vermilion and gold
autumn's reflection

Ohayo Haiku

down they flutter
in a cascade of color
rustle under feet

Ohayo Haiku

in fall yards and fields,
blossoms of blue, white, and red
~political placards

Peace

和

Ohayo Haiku

soft white feathers
drift slowly down covering
silent earth

Ohayo Haiku

fragile trees of glass
pristine whiteness covers earth
nature's artistry

Ohayo Haiku

bird's nest in tree,
protected by summer's leaves
now vulnerable

Ohayo Haiku

walking swiftly through
an icy, barren wasteland
~Ohio's tundra

Ohayo Haiku

silvery winter
snowflakes swirl in air
December delights

Ohayo Haiku

the sun bursts through
golden streaks from silver clouds
January's dawn

Ohayo Haiku

red streaks in the sky
broaden to wide patches
a winter dawn

Ohayo Haiku

angel in the snow
stands guard and protects
loved ones

Ohayo Haiku

the fog fades
elk and bison appear
grazing by the stream

Ohayo Haiku

yolk encased in white
breaks away and becomes
exquisite sunrise

Ohayo Haiku

black bundle of fur
with eyes bright, reflexes quick
gentle purr that soothes

Ohayo Haiku

rare you are
often thought of, desired
bountiful loving

Ohayo Haiku

a soft gentle kiss
becomes demanding, probing
and I am consumed

Ohayo Haiku

hugs become
gentle kisses demanding
love's consummation

www.ingramcontent.com/pod-product-compliance
Lightning Source LLC
Chambersburg PA
CBHW031427040426
42444CB00006B/716